BoldLeads Reviews Ways to Growth Hack Real Estate

By BoldLeads, Michael Mally and
Michele Frazier

Table of Contents

How to Prepare for Success

It's no secret that preparation is an absolutely fundamental component of success in any industry, and this is especially true when it comes to achieving success as a real estate agent. It is likewise the case that few people enter the real estate industry with no intention of working diligently or preparing appropriately, yet many agents will still struggle and ultimately fail to secure a foothold in the world of real estate. In the overwhelming majority of these circumstances, failure is not caused by a lack of effort in preparing to succeed, but is rather the result of a total lack of understanding when it comes to the most ideal preparatory strategies for yielding success.

When I founded BoldLeads, I did so based on a real estate adage that I feel is incredibly accurate and reflects a fundamental truth about what it takes to succeed in the real estate industry. The adage is as follows:

"Most agents don't fail because they can't sell a house. Most agents fail because they can't get clients."

The most successful agents are those who understand how important it is to have a consistently replenishing pipeline of clients, which is why so many agents are in tireless pursuit of any new lead that has the slightest potential of eventually being converted to a listing.

Adopting the Ideal Mindset

The most outstanding real estate agents all share a similar mindset that pushes them to endlessly chase after leads while using established practices and testing out new strategies in the hope of improving their efficiency in some way. This mindset ensures continual progress toward greater levels of efficiency so that agents are able to generate more and more leads as they hone their own strategies and incorporate newly developed ones into their approach.

Through early adoption of newly developed strategies and programs along with the understanding that improved efficacy in lead generation represents an opportunity for a lucrative and long-term return on investment, real estate agents put themselves in an excellent position to succeed for many years to come. Of course, this requires agents to routinely step outside of their comfort zone, but this is absolutely necessary in order to avoid falling behind in the use of best practices.

Creating an Essential Real Estate Toolbox

Real estate agents who understand the necessity of adopting an ideal mindset also know that there are certain tools that are critical to success, including each of the following:

- CRM
- Google calendar
- Landing page tool
- Email/SMS auto-responder
- Facebook/Google account

In the chapters that follow, I will discuss how these tools can be used in the implementation of an effective and outside-the-box strategy for improved lead generation and a greater likelihood of achieving sustainable and long-term real estate success.

Getting More Listings

Understanding the Mindset of Potential Sellers

Understanding the mindset of potential sellers in conjunction with the strategies most likely to generate a desired response is particularly critical when it comes to generating real estate success. This means that real estate agents must be able to differentiate between the many types of sellers and understand how to develop a strategic plan that properly leverages each potential seller's individual circumstances. The types of sellers an agent is most likely to encounter are as follows:

• Distressed sellers
• Empty nesters
• Sellers motivated by a significant life event (e.g., death or divorce)

• Sellers interested in testing the market to see if their home will sell

Considering the fact that lead generation is essentially the lifeblood of the real estate industry, agents have to develop clear strategies designed to attract the attention of each kind of seller. While specific strategies based on each individual seller's unique circumstances are indeed effective, there are several approaches that consistently draw the attention of sellers regardless of circumstance and allow the agent to operate in a far more efficient fashion. These approaches include sharing useful, updated information regarding the seller's home, such as:

• Home values and listing prices
• Real estate market data
• Factors that positively or negatively influence home value

• Local real estate market activity

With a deep understanding of the information that is most likely to draw the attention of potential sellers, real estate agents are better able to develop and implement consistently effective strategies for generating leads and securing listings.

Development and Implementation of Consistently Effective Strategies

Real estate agents often generate exceptional results through the use of strategies designed to properly leverage the information potential sellers tend to be most interested in. Through the use of marketing strategies that offer the prospective client access to specific information about their home, agents are able to collect a great deal of information about the potential seller and therefore increase the likelihood of securing a future listing. The following types of marketing offers tend to be most effective in this regard:

- "What's your home worth?"
- Local market reports
- "We buy houses for cash"
- Local success stories
- "Avoid these common seller mistakes"
- Commission rebates

These strategies are particularly effective when they send the potential client to a well-designed landing page that includes a variety of helpful features, such as automated comparative market analysis. While these techniques are established and effective in generating leads and converting potential clients into listings, there are always new strategies being developed for use. For example, I have used the "Make Me Move" feature on

Zillow to generate countless free seller leads, which I recently discussed in great detail at the following link:http://boldleads.com/generate-free-seller-leads-zillow/.

Getting More Buyers

Understanding the Mindset of Potential Buyers

As you may have noticed, understanding what motivates real estate agents to succeed, sellers to sell and buyers to buy is of critical importance, and it is for this reason that I have placed so much emphasis on the need to understand the mindset of buyers and sellers alike. Just as there are different kinds of sellers, so too are there many different kinds of homebuyers, so real estate agents have to understand how to develop and implement strategies that successfully draw the attention of potential homebuyers and effectively stimulate interest in the agent's available listings.

What Gets the Attention of a Homebuyer?

There are a number of tried-and-true strategies for getting the attention of a homebuyer through varied marketing concepts as well as specific types of content or services offering the kind of information typically valued by prospective homebuyers. These strategies are often centered on providing the following promotional offers and information:

• Lists of homes
• Hot deals
• Rebates
• Free giveaways
• Off-market properties
• Individual properties
• Online home search

While the nature of the offers and information is certainly critical in generating initial interest from homebuyers, there are other factors that must be considered in yielding the greatest possible degree of success in securing homebuyer leads. Getting the attention of the homebuyer is merely the first step of the process, and converting that attention into useful buyer leads requires additional focus on the part of the real estate agent.

Utilizing Effective Landing Pages and Five New Techniques for Capturing Buyer Leads

When an agent has effectively piqued the interest of a potential homebuyer though the offer of information relating to lists of available homes, off-market properties, hot deals and the like, the next step requires securing the potential homebuyer lead through the use of an effective landing page. It is important to recognize that not all landing pages are equally efficient when it comes to capturing buyer leads, so it is best to utilize one that can secure as much useful information regarding the prospective client even if they forget to submit a completed form or fail to include otherwise relevant information.

Of course, having information that will pique the interest of a potential homebuyer is only useful when it is able to reach the potential homebuyer, so each of the following techniques can be utilized to ensure the most appropriate level of exposure:

• Adwords campaigns
• Craigslist posts
• YouTube ads
• Facebook ads
• Open houses

Through the use of these strategies, real

estate agents are able to continuously generate new leads in the most efficient way possible. With a consistent pipeline of clients always in place, real estate agents can enjoy a greater degree of success due to an adherence to a philosophy in which it is clearly best to "work smarter, not harder."

Growth Hacks for Rapid Increases in Leads: Local Exposure and Gross Commissions

Identifying Priorities to Ensure Efficient Use of Advertising Strategies

Few real estate agents are so fortunate that they can simply use an unlimited advertising budget to saturate the market without any regard for carefully targeting a specific audience or developing efficient methods for generating leads and securing listings. Even if you had the benefit of an unlimited marketing budget, it would be unbelievably wasteful to operate in this way and would likely turn away a fairly substantial number of potential clients.

This is why it is important to use your

advertising budget on strategies that will actually work and will also contribute to the continual development of your wholly positive reputation as a real estate professional. After all, part of any advertising strategy involves selling clients on the idea of working with you due to your excellent judgment and expertise, which means that you have to carefully control the message you send to potential clients at all times.

A New Spin on Old School Methods

The real estate industry has a long history of widely varying techniques that have been used by real estate agents over the years, and many of those techniques are still quite useful today. Real estate agents who put a spin on these techniques in order to better reflect the present day can yield consistently impressive results that are exceptionally effective in driving interest among both buyers and sellers.

Webinar hosting is one example that has proved to be particularly effective, and this strategy is nothing more than a simple twist on the old-school seminar technique that is actually still quite prevalent among professionals in the real estate industry. The difference with a webinar is that it is far more convenient for you and the leads currently in your database, and it is even possible to record the webinar so anyone unable to attend can still view it at a later date and time.

There are a number of other strategies that are similarly able to achieve consistently exceptional results when properly utilized, including each of the following:

• Automating FSBOs with IFTTT

- Craigslist/Make Me Move
- Exit-Intent technology
- Simplified approach to direct mail
- Choosing a neighborhood farm with a turnover rate greater than five percent

These strategies are only the beginning, and it is equally important to implement a social media marketing campaign in order to reach a broader audience within the younger demographic. Instagram and other social media platforms all represent cost-efficient methods for courting substantial future growth and enhanced professional recognition, so they ought to be used with great frequency to ensure a continually replenishing pipeline of future clients.

Converting Leads Into Clients

Sales Techniques 101

Obviously, the goal of generating a substantial number of leads is to convert the greatest possible percentage of those leads into clients. As a real estate agent, you are likely already well aware of the fact that this requires a great deal of salesmanship on your part, and, for many agents, this means becoming comfortable with being uncomfortable. Of course, a balanced approach in which you remain persistent but not overbearing is best, and it is also unbelievably helpful to have as much information about the lead as possible before following up on any indication of interest.

There are several ways to research

information regarding the lead before making contact, including though the use of Spokeo, Rapportive and a number of other similar services. This research can supplement the information you collect through your landing page in order to get a fairly accurate vision of the client and to understand how to tailor your sales techniques in the most appropriate fashion.

In addition to performing research, it is also helpful to remain organized and on-task through the use of customer relationship software, or CRM. These systems often serve as the foundation for a real estate agent's marketing strategies, so it is critical to utilize an ideal CRM system to ensure you are able to operate in the most efficient way possible.

Phone, SMS and Email Techniques

The speed with which you respond to potential clients is absolutely critical when it comes to converting leads to actual clients. This is especially the case if you are using an automated system that reaches out to the client after they indicate their interest through your landing page or some other prompt you have set up. In order to ensure the greatest level of success, you should have a script prepared for all of the various circumstances in which a potential client may reach out to you, including one for buyers and another for sellers.

This script should be modified according to the method of communication being used, whether it is phone, text message, SMS or email, and the conversation should always be kept brief and should focus on arranging an appointment time in which you can meet with the client in the manner that is most convenient for them. Make sure to ask leading questions and to focus on developing a sense of trust with the client, as the early establishment of trust is often the most critical determining factor when it comes to converting a lead into a client.